A Mother holds you by the hand
Some of the time
And by the heart
All of the time.

A

Mother

holds you by the heart...

Words for mothers from the 19th and 20th centuries
Collected by Beryl Peters

Copper Beech Publishing

First published in Great Britain by
Copper Beech Publishing Ltd
© Copyright Beryl Peters 1994

ISBN 1 898617 02 3

A CIP catalogue record for this book is available from the British Library.

Copper Beech Publishing Ltd
P.O. Box 159, East Grinstead
Sussex RH19 4FS England

'Simply having children does not make mothers...'

*All around the world people are being 'mothered'
by someone special to them.
This book is dedicated to Winifred Alice Peters,
someone special to me, my mother in law who,
in the absence of my natural mother, has been
a worthy substitute and a true friend.*

Beryl Peters

Where there is a mother in the house,
matters speed well.

❦

The mother's heart is the child's classroom.

❦

The best mothers
help you put down roots
then offer you the gift of wings.

Men are what their mother's made them.

⁕

All that I am
Or hope to be
I owe to my angel mother.

⁕

Simply having children
does not make mothers.

⁕

Mother is the name for God in the lips and hearts
of little children.

*A good mother and health
are a child's wealth.*

A Mother's Work - Patching

(i)

A mother has the power and the wish to do
Some noble deed, a labour great and true;
But the work at hand - my work, I knew -
Was patching, only patching.

(ii)

At first, it seemed my way was barred
To higher things; to mend the marred
Was not for me: it was so simple - and so hard -
This patching, only patching.

(iii)

But in due time, as day by day
I saw the need, I learned the way
Life planned for me, and came to say -
Though 'twas patching, only patching.

(iv)
Some must mend while others make,
Some must join what others break,
And the nearest work is the work I'll take,
Though 'tis patching, only patching.

(v)
So now I patch the breaks and tatters life is sending,
Every day: all the poor old fragments mending,
Clothes, hearts, failed plans, and crookt lives blending,
All want patching, only patching.

Don't aim to be an earthly saint,
with eyes fixed on a star,
Just try to be the fellow
that your mother thinks you are.

✤

A mother
who boasts two boys
was ever accounted rich.

✤

Youth fades, love droops,
the leaves of friendship fall:
A mother's secret love outlives them all.

A mother's love is mighty,
but a mother's heart is weak,
And by it's weakness overcomes.

The bravest battle that ever was fought;
Shall I tell you where and when?
On the maps of the world you will find it not;
It was fought by the mother of men.

A MOTHER'S CARE.

Is not a young mother
one of the sweetest sights
life shows us?

Children
are the anchors that hold a mother to life.

❦

He that would the daughter win
Must with the mother first begin.

❦

They say there is no other
Can take the place of mother.

❦

A mother is like an octopus -
always tentacles enough to reach all her offspring.

My mother is like a chocolate cream
To others she is firm
But I know her soft heart.

Mother's Old Cookery Book

(i)

Its pages are stained, and written o'er
With careless pencil and pen,
Its leaves are ragged, its back is bent,
It will never look neat again.

(ii)

But oh! the dainties it helped to make,
In the busy summer morning;
Or the Christmas pudding, or wedding cake,
All unknown rules a-scorning.

(iii)

Here are buns Ned likes so well,
Here is Father's favourite pie,
And many recipes seem to tell
When Mother's skill was nigh.

(iv)

Many a festal day it crowned,
Many a Sunday dinner,
Many a washing-day meal it found -
Food for the saint or sinner.

(v)

So I think, no matter how choice my books,
Well bound, or clearly printed
(Set on the shelves for the sake of looks,
As I have heard it hinted).

(vi)

Or comforting friends for a lonely hour,
In a cosy ingle nook,
I still must value, and own the power
Of this useful little book.

Like mother, like daughter,
Like hen, like chicken.

❧

Who takes the child by the hand,
takes the mother by the heart.

❧

An ounce of mother is worth a pound of clergy.

No one but doctors and mothers
know what it's like to have interruptions!

❦

The successful mother sets her children free
and becomes more free herself in the process.

❦

The mother is a matchless beast.

✻

Thank you for teaching me your
three grand essentials for happiness:
Something to do
Something to love
Something to hope for.

✻

A mother's truth
keeps constant youth.

❧

Ten thousand parks where deer do run,
- Ten thousand roses in the sun,
Ten thousand pearls beneath the sea,
My mother more precious is to me.

❧

Mother, you make the best of everything
Think the best of everybody
Hope the best for your children.

One may desert one's father,
Though he be a high official,
But not one's mother,
Though she be a beggar.

❧

No bones are ever broken
by a mother's beating.

❧

In the eyes of the mother
every beetle is a gazelle.

❧

Father has his will, but Mother has her way!

Mother - House Weary

(i)

I'm going out! I'm tired of tables, chairs;
I'm tired of walls that hedge me all about;
I'm tired of rooms and ceilings, carpets, stairs,
   And so - I'm going out!

(ii)

Somehow or other, what I need today,
Are skies and birds that carol, winds that shout!
I want Dame Nature's friendship. Thus I say,
   Good-bye - I'm going out!

(iii)

It's just house tiredness. Trivial humdrum strain!
But when I've climbed the hill, no doubt
   I'll long to hurry back again, as
   Home thoughts flood my mind.

A wise mother
is one who has a great deal to say -
and remains silent.

❦

The highest duties of life are found
Lying upon the lowest ground
In hidden and unnoticed ways
In mother's works on common days.

❦

Which is the favourite word with mother?
- the last one!

Oh! the gladness of a mother when she's glad,
Oh! the sadness of a mother when she's sad,
But the gladness of her gladness,
Or the sadness of her sadness,
Is as nothing to her madness
When she's mad!

There is in all this world
no fount of love
so strong as that within
a mother's heart.

Who fed me from her gentle breast
And hushed me in her arms to rest
And on my cheeks sweet kisses pressed?
My Mother

When sleep forsook mine open eyes
Who was it sang sweet lullaby
And rocked me so that I would not cry?
My Mother

Who ran to help me when I fell
And would some pretty story tell
Or kiss the place to make it well?
My Mother

A Mother's Heart Treasures

There is a treasure spot where women keep
Heart treasures locked away;
They take them out sometimes, when shadows creep
At twilight time of day.

Strangers would look at them in mute surprise,
They'd never, never guess
Wherein the beauty of those treasures lies -
Their worth and preciousness.

A meadow walk; vows old but fresh and clear;
A kiss; love's ecstasy;
Laughter of children: such the flotsam dear
On which they turn the key!

Go my son and shut the shutter,
This I heard the mother utter.

The shutter's shut the boy did mutter
I can't shut it any shutter!

Baby's Skies

Would you know the baby's skies?
Baby's skies are mamma's eyes;
Mamma's eyes and smiles together
Make the baby's pleasant weather.

Mamma keep your eyes from tears,
Keep your heart from foolish fears;
Keep your lips from dull complaining,
Lest the baby think 'tis raining.

Mother, whene'er I think of you...

Sweet memories of many happy days
Of friendly chats upon sequestered ways,
Of loving sympathy and helpful praise
Come to me down the years like morning dew,
Mother, whene'er I think of you.

Mother's Work

Sewing on buttons, overseeing rations,
Soothing with a kind word others' lamentations,
Guiding clumsy Bridgets, coaxing sullen cooks,
Entertaining company and reading recent books.

Mother says "Forget It"

My children, if people pass you by
With their noses in the sky,
Just you wink the other eye -
Forget it!

If you hear what people say,
Things about you - let them say
Go serenely on your way -
Forget it!

When your trouble's big and deep,
Shut it out of doors and sleep,
Spilt milk shouldn't make you weep
Forget it!

The Medicine Bottle

Jennie:
"Yes, this is my medicine bottle,
Mamma sent me up stairs to find
It's all very well for my mother
But I think it's really unkind.

To make me take stuff that is bitter
And horrid to swallow, dear me!
If I were a little girl's mother
What a different mother I'd be."

Mamma:
"Ah Jennie, 'tis fortunate, truly
That you're but a dear little girl
With eyes like the bluest of violets,
And soft golden hair all a-curl.

And that mother is wise in her training
And 'spite of your tears and your frown
When your cough is so bad and you need it
Makes you swallow your medicine down."

Mother and Daughter

Sad it is mothers and daughters must part again,
Ere of their meeting they've felt the full bliss
E'en as I'm speaking the tears quickly start again,
As I remember how short the time is.
Foolish am I! My tears quickly drying,
With kisses and smiles
let me welcome you home.

Now is no moment for weeping and sighing
These are the holidays; daughter has come!
These are the holidays -
Brightest and best of days!
Daughter has come!

Mothers know
The way to rear up children (to be just)
They know a simple, merry, tender knack,
Of tying sashes, fitting baby-shoes,
And stringing pretty words that make no sense,
And kissing full sense into empty words,
Which things are corals to cut life upon,
Although such trifles.

A mother is like a sunny day
casting brightness around her children
warming them while they are close
still shining from far away.

Nobody Knows but Mother

How many buttons are missing today?
Nobody knows but mother.
How many playthings are strewn in her way?
Nobody knows but mother.

How many thimbles and spools has she missed?
How many burns on each fat little fist?
How many bumps to be cuddled and kissed?
Nobody knows but mother.

How many cares does a mother's heart know?
Nobody knows but mother.
How many joys from her mother-love flow?
Nobody knows but mother.

How many prayers by each little white bed?
How many tears for her babes has she shed?
How many kisses for each curly head?
Nobody knows but mother.

A Lesson for Mamma

Dear mamma, if you just could be
A tiny little girl like me,
And I your mamma, you would see
How nice I'd be to you.
I'd always let you have your way;
I'd never frown at you and say,
'You are behaving ill to-day;
Such conduct will not do.'

I'd never say, 'Well, just a few!'
I'd let you stop your lessons, too;
I'd say, 'They are too hard for you,
Poor child, to understand.'
I'd put the books and slates away;
You shouldn't do a thing but play.
And have a party every day.
Ah-h-h, wouldn't that be grand!

My mother is like my favourite book
she can always be consulted
she never commands.

*My mother gives much away,
but she always keeps her temper.*

Motherhood
- all love begins and ends there.

❦

Mother's Work

Toiling at noon, like a busy bee,
Teaching the little ones A, B, C;
Hearing the older ones read and spell,
Smiling and praising when all was well;
Washing and brushing 'twixt work and play,
Such is the mother's work, day by day.

❦

What is a coach without a horse?
What is a home without a mother?

My Little Daughters

I have a little daughter; she is good as gold,
So loving to her mother, always does as she is told.
I love to hear her laughing as she runs about the house;
But when mother has a headache she is quiet as a mouse.

I have a little daughter as cross as she can be,
Such a worry to her mother, that anyone can see -
So tiresome and noisy as she runs in and out;
A very naughty little girl, of that there is no doubt.

My best of little daughters, I hope you'll with me stay,
For, when you do, the other one is sure to keep away.
She's really such a torment I do not want her near;
I'd rather be without her, so please stay with me dear.

About these little daughters - they both have but one name;
The bad one and the good one are really just the same.
I've only got one daughter, as I dare say you have guessed;
But now you know for certain, because I have confessed!

Lines to Kathleen from her Mother

As sure as on your wedding day
A broom to you I'll send
In sunshine use the brushing side,
In storms the other end!

❦

Every grouse shakes this house,
Every grumble makes it crumble
But loving words and kindly deeds,
Will give it all the strength it needs.

Hundreds of stars in the pretty sky,
Hundreds of shells on the shore together
Hundreds of birds that go singing by,
Hundreds of birds in the sunny weather.

Hundreds of dewdrops to greet the dawn
Hundreds of bees in the purple clover,
Hundreds of butterflies on the lawn
But only one mother the wide world over.

I can't resolve
One thing or other
Until I've first
Consulted mother.

❧

A mother understands what a child does not say.

❧

My Mother's Blessing To Her Children

Thine be every joy and treasure,
Peace, enjoyment, love and pleasure.

A mother is a special treasure
full of love without measure.

No matter how old a mother is, she watches her
middle-aged children for signs of improvement.

Florida Scott-Maxwell (Suffragette)

Time's Changes - 1892

In days of old, so the chronicles say,
Maids helped their mother in a household way,
Now times have changed; the maid for culture wishes
And reads her book while mother cleans the dishes.

Mother's Timetable

On Monday,
wash your heart and rinse your cares away,
On Tuesday,
iron out harsh thoughts, till they are smooth and gay,
On Wednesday,
dust tired thoughts, and polish up your smiles,
On Thursday,
sort out kindly deeds and place them in neat piles,
On Friday,
think of friends and pleasant things to do,
On Saturday,
clear up your cares, and mend up moods of blue,
On Sunday,
look around and see what you have done,
And pray the week has been well spent, and another
well begun.

Abridged

Her mother named her "Mary", that good
old-fashioned name,
And all through school she wore it, contented
with the same;
But when she'd finished learning, and left the
school behind,
She dropped the "r" and "May" became
-'twas so much more refined.
She's married now and off the hands of her
enduring pa,
Still more her name has been reduced -
her youngest calls her "Ma".

❋

Mother's love is like old slippers
Which are caressing, but do not bind
- too worn by time closely to cling
spoil our happiness or fret our mind.

❦

Mother's Advice

A good thought is worth untold gold;
A good deed is priceless.

Late for breakfast
hurried for dinner
cross at tea.

Consider the postage stamp - it's usefulness consists in its
ability to stick to one thing until it gets there!

A cheerful spirit gets on quick;
A grumbler in the mud will stick.

No star is ever lost we once have seen,
We always may be what we might have been.

Mother's Advice

Too much learning hinders knowledge
A room may be so full of furniture that you can hardly
find a chair to sit down on.

A handful of help
Is worth a cartload of pity.

There is skill in all things -
even in making porridge!

Beryl Peters collects autograph albums, friendship books and other antiquarian sources of writing of people keeping a record of their lives.

From her various collections she has compiled this book in an effort to revitalise these captivating words which were written so long ago.

Whereas much of the contents of this dedication to motherhood has been culled from her autograph albums, she acknowledges that many of the entries would have been copied from periodicals and postcards and then personalised for friendship's sake ..... some of them, therefore, deviate from the originals and can not be credited.

Material is taken from the early 1800s onwards when these personal messages were penned with loving care to be passed down in families from generation to generation.

Every effort has been made to trace ownership of the material used in this collection. If any omission has occurred it is inadvertent and it should be brought to the attention of the publisher.

Other Copper Beech Gift Books include:

Etiquette for Gentlemen
Rules for 'perfect behaviour' for the gentleman in every woman's life.

Mangles Mops & Feather Brushes
Advice for the laundry and cleaning the old-fashioned way.

How To Entertain Your Guests
A book of traditional indoor games originally collected in 1911.

The Duties of Servants
A look at the above and below stairs life 100 years ago.

The Ladies Oracle
"Shall I soon be courted?" "May I hope to receive a fortune?"
The answers to these and other questions can be found
by consulting this 1857 ladies oracle.

Other Copper Beech Gift Books include:

Poetry Thoughts & Merry Jests
Words of friendship from Victorian and Edwardian Autograph Albums.

Love is like a Mutton Chop...
Wry words of love, 1840-1940

Hand-me-down Wisdom
A book of treasured words
'The threads of wisdom bind us all, generation to generation, they are
written in autograph books, passed down in classrooms, kitchens, on
chance meetings and in so many other ways...'

Chains of Wisdom
More hand-me-down wisdom collected from people in the public eye.

The Extremely Useful Book of Christmas Lists
Lists for cards, gifts, reminders, menu planners, Christmas customs.
Everything you need to plan a successful festive celebration - and a
book small enough to carry in your handbag or pocket.

For your free catalogue write to
Copper Beech Publishing Ltd
P O Box 159, East Grinstead, Sussex RH19 4FS England

Copper Beech Gift Books
are designed and printed
in Great Britain